Witness History Series

THE ORIGINS OF WORLD WAR 1

Stewart Ross

The Bookwright Press
New York · 1989

Titles in this series

China since 1945
The Cold War
The Origins of World War I
The Russian Revolution
South Africa since 1948
The Third Reich

Cover illustration: Austria, Bulgaria and Turkey struggle
for power in the Balkans, 1908

First published in the
United States in 1989 by
The Bookwright Press
387 Park Avenue South
New York, NY 10016

First published in 1988 by
Wayland (Publishers) Ltd
61 Western Road, Hove
East Sussex BN3 1JD, England

Library of Congress Cataloging-in-Publication Data
Ross, Stewart
   The origins of World War I.

   (Witness history)
   Bibliography: p.
   Includes index.
   1. World War, 1914–1918 – Causes – Juvenile literature.
I. Title.   II. Series.
D511.R85   1989   940.3'11   88–24269
ISBN 0–531–18260–6

Typeset by Kalligraphics Limited, Horley, Surrey
Printed by Sagdos, S.p.A., Milan

Contents

Assassination   4

The Great Powers

The Triple Alliance   6
The Dual Alliance   8
The British Empire   10

International tension

Economic rivalry   12
Competing empires   14
The military buildup   16

The Triple Entente

Britain takes sides 1900-08   18
The end of British isolation   20
The Entente Cordiale   22
A second entente   24

The Balkans

Great Power rivalry 1908-14   26
A powder keg   28
Mounting tension   30
The First Balkan War   32
The Second Balkan War   34
Talk of war, 1914   36

The path to war

From Sarajevo to war 1914   38
The ultimatum   40
The Schlieffen Plan   42
A scrap of paper   44
World War   46

Why did it happen?

Can anyone be blamed?   48
How far back?   50
The causes   52

Leading figures   54

Important dates   56

Glossary   58

Further reading   60

Notes on sources   61

Index   62

Assassination

GAVRILO PRINCIP, a lean and sickly-looking young man, had been born in Bosnia, which is now part of modern Yugoslavia, in 1894. Fourteen years later his native land was swallowed up by the giant Austro-Hungarian Empire. Princip became obsessed with the idea of striking a dramatic blow for the freedom of his country and the Slav peoples in general. In 1912 he joined the Black Hand group of terrorists who were trained and supported by Serbia, Bosnia's independent Slav neighbor. Then, while continuing his studies in both Bosnia and Serbia, he awaited his moment. At last, in June 1914, the chance came.

Archduke Franz Ferdinand was heir to the throne of the Austro-Hungarian Empire. He felt it his duty to inspect the far-flung corners of his inheritance, especially if they were proving troublesome. On June 28, 1914, he and his wife, Sophie, arrived in the Bosnian capital of Sarajevo. Members of the Black Hand were waiting for them.

At about 10 a.m. the Archduke and his wife left the railroad station and drove in a procession of four open cars along the Appel Quay toward the town hall. In the clear summer sunshine six members of the Black Hand stood at intervals along the way, prepared to attack. In the event, only two

Gavrilo Princip shooting Archduke Franz Ferdinand and his wife, Sophie, on June 28, 1914. These few shots set in motion a chain of events that, in only a few weeks, led to world war.

had the nerve to act. The first was Nedeljko Cabrinovik. As the royal procession passed, he flung a bomb. It rolled off the Archduke's car, but a rear wheel was blown off the one following, wounding a soldier. After a brief delay the three remaining cars swiftly continued to the town hall, while police arrested Cabrinovik. At first Princip was not sure what had happened, but he hung around Schiller's café on the Quay hoping for an opportunity to attack if the procession returned that way.

A while later Princip was presented with the chance he had been waiting for. The leading car, followed by the Archduke's, made a wrong turn into the narrow Franz

In October 1915, over a year after the war started, Bulgaria declared war on the weakened Serbia. Bulgaria had a disappointing lack of success, and Serbian peasants who had fled from the Bulgarian forces were able to return home.

Josef Street next to the café. As they were backing out, Princip stepped forward and fired two shots at close range. Blood spurted from Franz Ferdinand's neck and his wife slumped forward. Within minutes they were both dead.

Four weeks later Austria–Hungary declared war on Serbia. Five weeks after the assassination the whole of Europe was at war. Never can two shots have had such far-reaching and horrifying consequences.

The Triple Alliance

IN 1900 THE GREATEST power in continental Europe was Germany. Yet the German Empire was comparatively new. It had been founded in 1871 from a number of independent German states that had united under Prussia to defeat the French in the short but dramatic Franco-Prussian War of 1870–71.

The emergence of a united Germany totally altered the political and economic map of Europe. Having destroyed French military superiority, the new power soon threatened Britain's industrial dominance. German armies were formidable; an impressive navy was under construction, and the nation had joined other European powers in gathering colonies in Africa and Asia to expand its empire worldwide. The man who had guided German unification and who oversaw the empire until 1890 was the Imperial Chancellor, Prince Otto von Bismarck.

After the Franco-Prussian war of 1870–71, Germany emerged as a major world power. French forces are seen here desperately fighting the invader outside Paris. For twenty years after this war German foreign policy tried to keep France isolated, thus frustrating any desire for revenge.

In foreign affairs his one overriding aim was to keep France isolated and friendless in Europe. He knew that France would seek revenge for the defeat of 1870–71 and the harsh terms that Germany had imposed. Not only had France lost the rich eastern province of Alsace and part of Lorraine to Germany, but it had also been forced to pay massive reparations. To isolate France, Bismarck arranged a series of alliances between the Emperors of Germany, Austria and Russia. In 1879 he drew up a binding treaty between Germany and Austria, an alliance that Italy joined in 1882. So the Triple

Alliance was formed.

Like Germany, Italy was a newly formed nation. Its unification had begun in 1859, but was completed only with the acquisition of Rome in 1870. In military and industrial terms, Italy was not nearly as powerful as Germany, but Bismarck saw the new alliance as a useful counterbalance to French ambitions in the Mediterranean and North Africa. Italy and Austria–Hungary also joined with Britain in 1887 to sign two Mediterranean Agreements whereby they undertook to safeguard each other's interests.

Austria–Hungary was less centralized than either Germany or Italy. Its empire covered a huge area of central Europe, from southern Poland in the north to the Balkans in the south, held together by the skillful rule of diplomats and civil servants in the capital, Vienna. Industrially, Austria–Hungary was still relatively underdeveloped, although its armies were large and feared by smaller neighbors. Austria's chief preoccupation was with the southern frontier, where it opposed both Slav independence and Russian ambition.

One important factor about the Triple Alliance is that following Bismarck's dismissal in 1890, the new German Emperor, Kaiser William II, was unable to keep France isolated. In 1894 France allied with Russia, thus presenting the Germans with the possibility of hostilities on two fronts.

Victor Emmanuel III, King of Italy 1900–46. Italian anxiety about French ambitions led them to join Bismarck's Triple Alliance System.

Otto von Bismarck (1815–98), the first Chancellor of the German Empire. He played a major part in the unification of Germany and in constructing the Triple Alliance with Austria–Hungary and Italy to isolate the French.

The Dual Alliance

From the time of Louis XIV (1643–1715) to the Franco-Prussian War of 1870–71, French armies had generally been regarded as the most powerful in Europe. In January 1812, Napoleon I commanded a European empire the like of which had not been seen since Roman times. Yet less than sixty years later, the French, under Napoleon III, had been crushed by the Germans. They were forced to witness the proclamation of a German Empire in Louis XIV's own Palace of Versailles, just outside Paris.

Although after the war the French had paid the massive reparations demanded by the Germans six months early, their hopes for revenge were futile as long as Bismarck remained in power. France had a sophisticated stock exchange and a large overseas empire, but in industrial terms lagged far behind Germany. Britain, France's traditional enemy, was suspicious of French colonial designs and unwilling to become entangled in European alliances. Italy and Austria–Hungary were allied to Germany. Of all the major European powers, only Russia remained as a potential ally for France.

Historically, France and Russia had been the bitterest of foes. Napoleon I's invasion of Russia in 1812 had marked the beginning of the end for his revolutionary empire; later the two nations had fought each other in the Crimea (1854–56). Moreover, France was, after 1870, a democratic republic. Russia was an absolutist state, ruled by a Czar who claimed that his power came directly from God. Opposition to him was ruthlessly, albeit inefficiently, suppressed. On the surface at least, nothing seemed more unlikely than a Franco-Russian alliance.

Nevertheless, the governments of France and Russia had one strong bond: both were

This picture shows the German Empire being formally proclaimed in the Palace of Versailles just outside Paris. This was a great humilation for the French, who had just been defeated by the Germans.

▲ The mighty German armament works of the Krupp family at Essen. By 1900 Germany had outstripped all European rivals in the production of iron and steel.

▼ Nicholas II, Czar of Russia, with his wife, Alexandra. The backward-looking Russian government had no great love for republican France, but they feared the new aggressive German Empire more. Thus the Russians and the French formed the Dual Alliance in 1894.

alarmed at the way the balance of power in Europe had been altered by the formation of the German Empire. Russia, with a population of 125 million, was potentially a devastating power. Its empire stretched from Poland in the west to the Pacific in the east, from the Arctic in the north to the borders of Persia (now Iran) in the south. But Russia was extremely backward technologically, and needed capital to industrialize. France was only too pleased to provide the necessary loans.

In the Balkans, where the Turkish Empire was dissolving fast, Russia came face to face with the other power seeking to move into the area: Austria–Hungary, the inseparable ally of Germany. Thus it was, to the surprise of many, that on January 4, 1894, France ended years of isolation and signed a defensive treaty with Russia. The Dual Alliance had been formed.

The British Empire

The famous Charge of the Light Brigade in the Crimean War, 1854–56. Although skilled in small colonial wars, the British Army was inexperienced when it came to large-scale conflict.

At the start of the twentieth century, Britain was the most isolated of the great European powers. To some extent this was the result of deliberate policy. Britain was essentially a naval and commercial power, its small armies scattered worldwide and totally unsuited to the sort of fighting that might take place on the mainland of Europe. Its brave but incompetent performance in the Crimean War pointedly illustrated this. In 1900 the British Navy was far larger than those of any two other powers combined, but this was not of immediate practical use for fighting a European war.

For the middle years of the nineteenth century, Britain enjoyed a period of unparalleled economic dominance. Having been the first country in the world to industrialize, British manufactured goods, in particular textiles, swamped world markets. Many of the raw materials for British industry came from an empire "on which the sun never set," an empire that included the Indian subcontinent, Canada, most of Australasia and huge tracts of Africa. On imperial maps proudly produced in London, one quarter of the world's land surface was colored red to show its allegiance to Queen Victoria.

Toward the end of the nineteenth century, however, British confidence began to crack. Newer and more efficient industries, in particular those of the United States and Germany, successfully challenged British supremacy. In the new technologies, such as electrical engineering and motorized transportation, Britain lagged behind. There were dangerous and ominous incidents overseas, too. In 1898 French and British forces came close to conflict at Fashoda, a disputed town on the upper Nile in the Sudan. The next year Britain became engaged in a humiliating war with the tiny Boer republics of the Orange Free State and the Transvaal in southern Africa. It took three years to defeat them, and all the while there was the possibility of other European colonial powers, led by Germany, forming a coalition against Britain.

As the century turned, Britain was reassessing its isolated position in the world. In 1898, the year of the Fashoda incident, a German Navy Law had announced a massive expansion of the German fleet. Britain also confronted Russian expansion toward India through Afghanistan and Persia. It was anxious, too, to limit Russian advances in the Balkans and Constantinople, which threatened the vulnerable Suez Canal, the main sea route to the Far East. Britain and its widespread empire could no longer afford to remain aloof and friendless in what was seen as an increasingly hostile world.

A Lancashire textile factory. For much of the nineteenth century, Britain was regarded as the "workshop of the world," sending its manufactured goods to every corner of the globe. Although not a great military nation, Britain had tremendous economic power.

Queen Victoria, who presided over the largest empire the world has ever seen. The Victorians proudly referred to it as "the empire on which the sun never set."

11

Economic rivalry

ONE OF THE COMMONEST causes of international tension can occur when nations come into conflict over commercial issues, such as those that divided Britain and Germany before World War I. During that period, politicians and writers in both countries exaggerated the conflict for political reasons, making the situation seem worse than it was.

The cartoon below shows Britain's anxiety at its declining commercial position in the world. It was ironically entitled "The Secret of Our Commercial Supremacy." It suggests that a general unwillingness to work hard was the cause of Britain's commercial problems. The cartoon opposite lays the blame on foreign imports.

This poster reflects the spirit of a movement, headed by the British politician Joseph Chamberlain, that tried to establish an area of free trade within the British Empire, protected from the competition of imported foreign goods by high customs tariffs. (Such a "free-trade" area is like the one formed by the European Ecomomic Community.) The position of the British

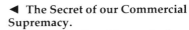

◄ **The Secret of our Commercial Supremacy.**
Clerk (to applicant for post of office-boy): "The guvnor's out. Call tomorrow at nine."
Applicant. "Oh, I say! Can't you make it later? I have my breakfast at nine."

► **Foreign goods on sale in Britain.**
John Bull: "Here, I say, this is a free country I know, but I'm not going to have your stalls right in front of my shop."

government was to support free trade with all countries. Free traders claimed that tariffs would raise the price of food and therefore give the British people only a "little loaf" to eat.

In the two British elections of 1910 the issue of free trade versus protectionism (known as Tariff Reform) received massive coverage. There was particular anxiety at the number of German imports, and this fueled talk of war. It is not difficult to find statistics that supported people's fears:

- In 1914 all the khaki dye for the uniforms of the British Army was manufactured in Germany.
- In 1900 Britain produced more coal than France, Germany, Russia, Austria–Hungary and Italy combined; by 1914 German production alone rivaled that of Britain.
- In early twentieth century, Britain – the founder of the modern railroad system and builder of many of the world's railroads – was shocked to learn of plans to link Berlin to Baghdad with a railroad line built or financed largely by Germany and its allies.

Yet:

- In June 1914 an Anglo-German agreement confirmed that the Berlin–Baghdad railroad would not threaten British interests in the Middle East.
- By 1914 Britain exported twice as many machine tools to Germany as were imported from German factories.
- British exports of coal to Germany doubled between 1904 and 1914.

In many fields cooperation between Britain and Germany was as marked as their rivalry. Therefore, perhaps commercial rivalry between the two nations was merely a symbol of a deeper hostility.

Competing empires

For a number of reasons, during the nineteenth century European powers seized many of the underdeveloped parts of the world as colonies. In Africa in the last quarter of the century, this process became a "scramble," each invader trying to seize territory before its rivals took it. By 1900 most of the continent had been divided up, but many tensions remained.

The map below shows which country had been most successful in the "scramble for Africa." At one time Cecil Rhodes, British Prime Minister of the Cape Colony of South Africa, talked of building a railroad that would run from Cape Town to Cairo on British territory all the way. But Germany's African colony blocked that dream. Compare this extract from a speech by Joseph Chamberlain in 1903 with the one below right made by a German historian in 1899:

Chamberlain
To my mind Britain has played a great part in the history of the world, and for that reason I wish Britain to continue. Then, in the second place, our object is . . . the realization of the greatest ideal which has ever inspired statesmen in any country or in any age – the creation of an Empire such as the world has never seen. We have to cement the union of the states beyond the seas; we have to consolidate the British race.[1]

The partition of Africa.

SPANISH MOROCCO · Algeciras
TUNIS
MOROCCO · Fez
Agadir ·
RIO DE ORO
ALGERIA
LIBYA
Cairo · Suez Canal
EGYPT
GAMBIA
FRENCH WEST AFRICA
PORTUGUESE GUINEA
SIERRA LEONE
LIBERIA
NIGERIA
Nile
FRENCH SOMALILAND
BRITISH SOMALILAND
ANGLO-EGYPTIAN SUDAN
ERITREA
Fashoda ·
ETHIOPIA
GOLD COAST
TOGO
CAMEROONS
FRENCH EQUATORIAL AFRICA
UGANDA
BRITISH EAST AFRICA (KENYA)
ITALIAN SOMALILAND
BELGIAN CONGO
GERMAN EAST AFRICA
Atlantic Ocean
ANGOLA
NORTHERN RHODESIA
MOZAMBIQUE
NYASALAND
GERMAN SOUTH WEST AFRICA
SOUTHERN RHODESIA
BECHUANALAND
MADAGASCAR
BOER STATES
· Cape Town
Indian Ocean

French
British
German
Portuguese
Belgian
Spanish
Italian
Anglo–Egyptian condominium

▲ The celebrated politician Joseph Chamberlain (1836-1914) who worked hard to build up the British imperial spirit. He is particularly remembered for his support of British expansion in Africa and for his campaign for tariff reform.

◀ A French cartoon drawn at the time of the Fashoda crisis of 1898. A French force moving across Africa from west to east reached the town of Fashoda on the Nile where they met British forces establishing a north-south route along the river.

German historian
We want to be a World Power and pursue colonial policy in the grand manner. ... Here there can be no step backward. The entire future of our people among the great nations depends upon it. We can pursue this policy with England or without England. With England means in peace; against England means – through war.[2]

England's hatred against us is inextinguishable; England is the enemy of yesterday, tomorrow, and forever.[3]

And at the time of the Fashoda crisis (1898) a French journalist had written:

Such ambitions and hostile attitudes were mirrored in Italy, Russia, Austria–Hungary and other colonial powers. The empires jealously eyed each other's advances throughout the world: in China, the Middle East, North Africa and, above all, in the Balkans.

The military buildup

Sir Edward Grey was British Foreign Secretary from 1906 to 1916. After the war he published his autobiography, in which he outlined what he thought had been the main cause of the conflict: "militarism and the armaments inseparable from it made war inevitable." He went on:

> *One nation increases its army and makes strategic railways towards the frontiers of neighbouring countries. The second nation makes counter-strategic railways and increases its army in reply. The first nation says this is very unreasonable, because its own military preparations were only precautions; the second nation says that its preparations also were only precautions, and points out . . . that the first nation began the competition; and so it goes on, till the whole Continent is an armed camp covered by strategic railways.[4]*

If Grey was right, and the armies went on expanding year by year, then in the end only war would bring the process to a halt. Ultimately, it was the countries with the largest populations that could continue expanding their armed forces the longest. The table below shows the numbers of men in 1914 ready to be mobilized in the event of war.

	Size of Army	Population (millions)
Triple Alliance		
German	2,200,000	65
Austria–Hungary	810,000	50
Italy	750,000	35
	3,760,000	150
Dual Alliance		
Russia	1,200,000	164
France	1,250,000	40
	2,450,000	204[5]

Factory workers assembling automatic 5-shot shotguns in 1911. Many people feared that the increased production of armaments and militarism made war inevitable.

▲ HMS *Dreadnought*, launched in 1906. This turbine-driven vessel revolutionized naval warfare; her speed and ten 12-inch guns set in turrets enabled her to sink an entire navy on her own. All existing ships were now obsolete and massive naval rebuilding programs began.

Admiral Alfred von Tirpitz (1849–1930), the German Minister of Marine from 1897 to 1916. It was Tirpitz who was largely responsible for making Germany a major naval power by the outbreak of World War I.

There was also a naval arms race before World War I, largely between Britain and Germany. In 1898 Germany had 13 battleships, Britain 29; but Germany passed a Navy Law in 1900 to increase its number to 38. Later, Britain planned to render all existing ships out of date with a new type of fast, heavily armed battleship, the dreadnought. By 1914 Germany had 37 battleships and Britain had 57, but both countries had several more dreadnoughts under construction. Sir Edward Grey had defended his country's position by stating, "Our navy is to us what the German Army is to Germany."[6] When Germany had started its naval building program, it declared that this was "to protect the Empire's sea trade and colonies."[7] The British politician Winston Churchill, on the other hand, regarded the German Navy as a "luxury."

So the countries of Europe had continued to build up their "defensive" armies and navies throughout the first thirteen years of the century. But would these forces preserve peace, or precipitate war?

Britain takes sides 1900–08

IN DIPLOMATIC TERMS, the most important European event during the first eleven years of the twentieth century was Britain's emergence from its isolated position of the 1890s. By 1902 the costly Anglo-Boer War had ended and Britain was tentatively looking for an ally to help undertake its worldwide commitments. In 1900 Admiral Tirpitz's Second German Navy Law had pledged to double the size of the German Navy by 1920, and Russia, one of Britain's colonial rivals, had occupied Chinese Manchuria.

After successful approaches toward Germany, Britain signed an alliance with Japan in January 1902. Later in the year the Triple Alliance (Germany, Austria–Hungary and Italy) was renewed, although the Italians also negotiated a secret treaty with the French. Anglo-French relations were much improved during 1903, assisted by a state visit of King Edward VII to Paris. In 1904 England and France came to an important agreement to settle their colonial differences, signing the Entente Cordiale. Meanwhile, fighting had broken out in Manchuria between Russia and Japan, resulting in humiliating defeat for the Russians in the Far East and revolution at home in 1905.

Germany came near to a double diplomatic success in the same year. Kaiser William II persuaded Czar Nicholas II of Russia to sign a treaty of alliance between their two countries at the Swedish island of Björkö, but this then was rejected by their politicians

Edward VII on his state visit to Paris in 1903. Britain and France had always mistrusted each other, but this visit marked a turning point in relations between the two neighbors.

A Japanese attack during the Russo-Japanese War of 1904-05. Britain had recently signed an alliance with Japan and was therefore pleased to note that the new ally was a considerable military power. The Russians were driven back in a number of battles, with massive losses.

and advisers at home. Germany also provoked France with a show of strength in Morocco, a country in which France claimed overriding influence. Britain stood by its new ally in this matter, and at the Algeciras Conference in 1906 Germany had to give way. To the Kaiser's annoyance, in 1911 Britain once more stood by France in the face of German aggression over Morocco.

Britain was now becoming more involved in European politics. In 1904 a total reorganization of the British Navy was begun by Sir John Fisher, with the big-gun battleship HMS *Dreadnought* being launched in 1906. This inspired Germany to widen the Kiel Canal between the North and Baltic seas in order to allow passage of bigger battleships, and to announce another Navy Law. Britain responded with an entente with Russia in 1907. The following year Russia could only watch as Austria–Hungary annexed the Balkan provinces of Bosnia and Herzegovina; an agreement made in return between Foreign Ministers Izvolsky of Russia and Aehrenthal of Austria, allowing Russia to sail warships through the Dardanelles, had met with widespread international displeasure. Even France failed to give support, and Russia had been forced to back down.

Meanwhile, in 1905 the German General Alfred von Schlieffen had finalized details of his plan whereby Germany would be able to fight a war on two fronts, against both Russia and France.

The end of British isolation

In the early twentieth century the world was changing fast. During the 1890s, British Prime Minister Lord Salisbury had declared that his foreign policy was to "drift lazily downsteam, occasionally putting out a boathook to avoid a collision." But the stream was now rougher, with rapids and whirlpools. It became clear that Britain could not navigate such waters alone. Conditions had changed.

- The Boer War, in which the British had taken three years to defeat two republics with a population smaller than that of a large European town, had revealed British military weakness.
- Germany had a policy of "Weltpolitik" ("world policy") – it wished to be an imperial power. The Berlin–Baghdad railroad was already under discussion.
- The United States, growing more powerful each year, would not tolerate British interference in its spheres of influence: South America and the eastern Pacific.
- The Dual Alliance of France and Russia, its chief colonial rivals, was of serious concern to Britain.
- An agreement with Germany to preserve China from foreign aggression collapsed when the Russians occupied Manchuria in 1900. Germany would not act against Russia, and Britain could do nothing on its own.
- Lord Salisbury, the author of Britain's independent line, resigned in 1902.

In Ostasien

(Zeichnung von Bruno Paul)

B

"Sie gestatten, Sir?"

This cartoon of 1900 shows Britain and Russia both trying to find a place in the profitable trade of the Far East. British and Russian interests clashed elsewhere, too, notably in Persia.

- In 1902 there was a revolt in Morocco, and French ambitions in the country threatened Britain's control of the Straits of Gibraltar.

But to whom could Britain turn? The Kaiser was quite clear about the matter:

Lord Salisbury is antiquated . . . England is short-sighted. Without alliances, her fate will be to be ultimately pressed out between Russia and the United States. With my army and your fleet that combination against us will be powerless.[8]

Joseph Chamberlain, the British Colonial Secretary, followed the same line:

. . . we should not remain permanently isolated on the continent of Europe, and I think that . . . the natural alliance is between ourselves and the great German Empire.[9]

In 1902 civil war broke out in Morocco. Both Britain and France were concerned lest the other should take advantage of the chaos to get a tighter grip on the country. In situations like this Britain needed an ally.

But it was not to be. The commercial, colonial and naval antagonism between Britain and Germany was too great. Instead, Britain withdrew from isolation with a more modest alliance. "The King," wrote Edward VII in 1901:

. . . considers it most essential that we should give Japan, when it is possible to do so, our hearty support on all occasions.[10]

By the treaty signed the following year, Britain and Japan defined their spheres of interest in the Far East and each agreed to help the other should they be attacked by more than one power.

21

The Entente Cordiale

In 1900 France was still considered Britain's chief adversary on the European continent. Despite their cooperation in the Crimea (1854–56), the Fashoda crisis (1898) had revived much of the old hatred between the two nations. Moreover, France was resentful of the British presence in Egypt. British forces had occupied that country in 1882 and remained there, despite strong French objections.

What lay at the heart of Anglo-French mistrust was in essence a simple matter.

1 Britain, being an island and without large armies, was consistently opposed to any major power dominating the continent, thus threatening Britain with invasion.

2 France throughout its history had been engaged in continual conflict with continental neighbors. Wherever success seemed assured, invariably Britain was found siding with France's enemies.

3 Since the eighteenth century a new dimension had been added to Anglo-French hostility, as each country competed to accumulate a worldwide empire. The Franco-Prussian War (1870–71) and

THE "IRREPRESSIBLE" TOURIST.

B-SM-RCK, "IT'M!—HA!—WHERE SHALL I GO NEXT?"

▲ This cartoon of 1885 from the British magazine *Punch* illustrates Britain's fears that Germany was rapidly developing into a world power.

▶ Kaiser William II's provocative visit to Morocco in 1905. William was deliberately testing France's Entente Cordiale, and was surprised and alarmed when Britain stood by its agreement, supporting French interests in Morocco.

the formation of the German Empire changed all this. Consider point 1 above in the light of this table:

The Relative Strengths of Germany and France (1914)
[Figures for population and army in millions]

	France	Germany
Population	40	60
Army (including reserves)	1.25	2.2
Battleships	25	37

Germany was now more likely to dominate Europe and thus worry Britain.

The only obstacle remaining in the path of an Anglo-French understanding was the colonial one (see point 3 above). The Entente Cordiale was:

> . . . nothing like an alliance. No enemy was singled out . . . No joint actions were planned. The entente was simply a settlement of colonial disputes that had been simmering for the last quarter-century.[11]

Essentially, the French recognized the British presence in Egypt, while Britain agreed to support its new friend's claims in Morocco.

But the Kaiser was not pleased. Edward VII wrote:

> The agreements that we have negotiated apart from him, without his permission and without his help, have stupefied him; they have produced in him a sense of isolation.[12]

Declaring,

> We have no reason to fear that our interests in Morocco can be overlooked or injured by any power,[13]

Kaiser William II challenged the Entente with a provocative visit to Morocco. France, supported by Britain, did not overreact, and at the Algeciras Conference in 1906 its position in Morocco was preserved. Sir Edward Grey, the British Foreign Secretary, later observed:

> The wind of armed German pressure . . . had in the long run only caused France to draw the cloak of the Entente with Britain more closely about her.[14]

But this made the European situation even more dangerous.

William II (1859–1941), Emperor of Germany before and during World War I. Britain and Germany seemed the natural allies in the early twentieth century, but mutual suspicion prevented an alliance between the two countries.

A second entente

In his autobiography, Sir Edward Grey explained why he considered an agreement between Russia and Britain to be highly desirable following the Entente Cordiale with France:

> *Russia was the ally of France; we could not pursue at one and the same time a policy of agreement with France and a policy of counter-alliances against Russia. . . . An agreement with Russia was the natural complement of the agreement with France; it was also the only practical alternative to the old policy of drift, with its continual complaints, bickerings, and dangerous friction.*[15]

The map below shows just where this "dangerous friction" occurred.

There were two strong objections to pursuing friendship with Russia. First, in Grey's own words, "Russian despotism was repugnant to British ideals."[16] The Czar, as absolute ruler, permitted no political opposition; his secret police wielded considerable power, and Jews and other minorities were continually persecuted. It did not seem right that Britain should make agreements with such a state.

Second, friendship between Britain, France and Russia would only increase the

Areas of European and Russian friction in Asia.

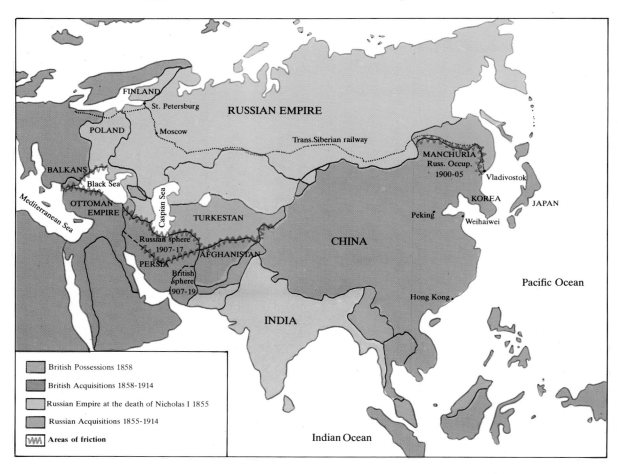

Legend:
- British Possessions 1858
- British Acquisitions 1858-1914
- Russian Empire at the death of Nicholas I 1855
- Russian Acquisitions 1855-1914
- Areas of friction

◄ Czar Nicholas II reviewing his armies. The Anglo-Russian Entente seriously alarmed Germany; a glance at a map of Europe makes it plain why Germany felt encircled.

▼ Sir Edward Grey (1862–1933), British Foreign Secretary from 1905 to 1916. Grey followed the Entente Cordiale with a similar agreement with Russia in 1907.

feeling of isolation felt by Germany since the Anglo-French Entente of 1904. While Britain remained outside the European alliance system, Germany was safe within the Triple Alliance. But now Germany was faced with a Triple Entente growing in power year by year. The Russian Sergei Sazonovo visited Germany in 1909 and witnessed German anger at the Anglo-Russian Entente of 1907:

> *Germany considered that this agreement, to which she was not a party, violated the principle of the open door [free access to Persian trade for all nations] and was injurious to her economic interests.*[17]

As long ago as 1885 the great German statesman Otto von Bismarck had warned that a union of France, Russia and Britain:

> *. . . would provide the basis for a coalition against us more dangerous for Germany than any other she might have to face.*[18]

Consequently, the Germans had been

encouraged when Britain and France failed to support Russia's wish to open the straits at the entrance to the Black Sea to its warships. In 1911 Germany again challenged French power in Morocco. French troops had occupied the city of Fez, contravening the 1906 Algeciras agreement. Germany sent a gunboat, the *Panther*, to protect its interests, but the Entente stood firm, and Germany backed down. Britain was hardly a neutral power any longer, but at what price for Europe?

Great Power rivalry 1908-14

THE TWO POWERS MOST concerned with the Balkans were Austria–Hungary and Russia. In 1897 they had reached an agreement to shelve their differences. This truce lasted until 1908, when Austria–Hungary annexed Bosnia and Herzegovina. Russia had agreed not to object to the seizure, on the understanding that its warships would be allowed to use the Dardanelles. As it happened, Russia received nothing in return.

Meanwhile, Britain had become increasingly worried by the growth of the German Navy, and a vigorous press campaign was mounted to build more dreadnoughts ("We want eight, and we won't wait"). At the same time, the two nations conducted a series of fruitless negotiations to try to halt their naval arms race. By 1910 these had collapsed. In 1911, Anglo-German relations deteriorated further with the mission of the German gunboat *Panther* to Agadir during the second Moroccan crisis. David Lloyd George, British Chancellor of the Exchequer, made a tough speech in which he warned that Britain could not accept peace at any price. Later in the year the Italians took advantage of Turkish weakness to invade Libya.

Another attempt by Britain to come to an understanding with Germany occurred in February 1912 when Lord Haldane, British Secretary of State for War, visited Berlin. When this mission failed, Britain and France reached an agreement on how their fleets would be best positioned for war with Germany.

War broke out in the Balkans in October 1912 when the newly formed Balkan League

Although a small country, Serbia was intensely nationalistic and had formidable armies. Here Serbian women are receiving military training. Measures such as this enabled Serbian forces to expand the size of their country considerably during the two Balkan wars 1912–13.

▲ The Italian flag being raised in Tripoli, the capital of Libya, in 1911. The Italian success in taking Libya from the Turks encouraged the Balkan countries to challenge successfully Turkish might the following year.

▼ A German *Unterseeboot*, or "U-boat." The Germans pioneered this new and devastating type of vessel, which the British, the leading naval power of the time, somewhat foolishly regarded as "cowardly."

(Greece, Serbia, Montenegro and Bulgaria) attacked and defeated Turkey. Although the Great Powers imposed a settlement in the Treaty of London (May 1913), a Second Balkan War broke out the following month. Serbia, Greece, Romania and Turkey turned on Bulgaria and deprived it of most of its gains. Peace was established at Bucharest in August, but the area became the center of international tension once more in November, when a German General, Liman von Sanders, was appointed Inspector-General of the Turkish Army.

Two Balkan wars had permitted Russia's Balkan ally, Serbia, to expand considerably, much to the irritation of Austria–Hungary and Germany. Therefore, the assassination of Franz Ferdinand in June 1914 seemed to present them with an ideal opportunity to put an end to Serbian ambitions forever.

A powder keg

It is common to describe the Balkans as the "powder keg of Europe," meaning it was an area likely to explode if not handled carefully. There were several reasons for this.

1. The Balkan peninsula was a very unstable area. Until well into the nineteenth century the Balkan states had been part of the Turkish Empire, which at one time had stretched from the gates of Vienna to southern Arabia. As Turkish power steadily declined, however, the people of the Balkans fought for their independence. Many were orthodox Christians who resented Muslim Turkish rule. Montenegro had never been wholly subdued by the Turks. The Greeks were the first to win their freedom. They were followed by Romania, Serbia and Bulgaria. Bosnia and Herzegovina were occupied by the Austrians and then annexed by them in 1908. This was the main cause of the friction between Serbia and Austria–Hungary.

The new Balkan states were proudly

The Balkans was an area of strategic importance to many countries. Around the turn of the century its shifting balance of power, with the increasing number of independent countries, made surrounding nations uneasy.

nationalistic and eager to expand their boundaries. Moreover, in the south of the peninsula there was a large area, covering Albania, Thrace and Macedonia, still under Turkish rule. Squabbling among the Balkan states, or between these states and Turkey, might have been less important had other powers not been involved, but of course this was not the case.

2. The map on the facing page shows the Balkans and the area surrounding it. The major powers all had their interests in the area:

Turkey. The Turks were still a powerful force in 1908, determined to hold on to their remaining European territory. The 1914 cartoon on the right, from the British magazine *Punch*, suggests how eager the Turks were to keep pace with the latest armaments, even though they could scarcely afford them. Their foreign trade was becoming increasingly dependent on Germany.

Italy. If Turkish power were to be reduced still further, then Italy had designs on both North Africa (Libya) and the eastern shore of the Adriatic. But this would not be viewed favorably by Austria–Hungary, Italy's partner in the Triple Alliance.

Austria–Hungary. The prime concern of Austria–Hungary was that Russia should not be permitted further influence in the Balkans. This aim would be best served by eliminating Serbia, Russia's Balkan ally.

Russia. Russia believed it had an historic mission to lead the Slavic people. This "Pan-Slav" concept provided an ideal excuse to interfere in the Balkans, many of whose people were Slavs, and to extend Russia's influence toward the eastern Mediterranean. Ideally, Russia wished to open the Dardanelles and Bosporus straits to its warships.

France and Britain. These two countries were torn between support for Russia, the third member of the Triple Entente, and a desire to see no major power threaten their commercial, naval and colonial interests in the eastern Mediterranean.

THE SPLENDID PAUPERS.

▲ Cartoon from the British magazine *Punch*, January 7, 1914: "The Splendid Paupers."
▼ Coronation of the new King of Serbia 1904. The proudly nationalistic Serbs were conceded full independence in 1878.

Mounting tension

Between 1908 and 1912 three factors made a major war more likely. These were the annexation of Bosnia and Herzegovina by Austria–Hungary; the escalation of the naval arms race between Britain and Germany; and the second Moroccan crisis of 1911. These three events left the major powers dissatisfied and hardened in their attitudes. War was now increasingly talked of as a possibility.

The German cartoon of 1911 below shows Kaiser William II attacking Agadir. Germany was forced to back down when England supported France's intervention in Morocco. This incident increased the antagonism Germany felt toward Britain.

Compare the mood of the German cartoon with the following extract from an Austrian article of 1909:

> *Never was a war more just. And never yet was our confidence in a victorious issue more firmly grounded.*
>
> *We are being driven into war: Russia drives us, Italy drives us, Serbia and Montenegro drive us, and Turkey drives us . . .*
>
> *Full of zest of battle the army awaits the tasks to which it is called.*[19]

Austria–Hungary did not go to war then, but such sentiments did little to foster European peace.

Farther east, similarly aggressive sentiments were harbored by the Russians, as demonstrated by their Foreign Minister,

The mailed fist at Agadir. A German cartoon of Kaiser William's arrogant intervention.

THE NEST IN DANGER

Sergei Sazonov:

Russia's historical mission – the emancipation of the Christian peoples of the Balkan peninsula from the Turkish yoke – was almost fulfilled by the beginning of the twentieth century . . . [Russia's] sole and unchanging object was to see that those Balkan people who had been freed by her age-long efforts and sacrifices should not fall under the influence of powers hostile to her . . . The Bosnia–Herzegovina crisis revealed with unmistakable clearness the aims of Austro-German policy in the Balkans and laid the foundation for an inevitable conflict between Germanism and Slavism.[20]

Sazonov's last sentence indicates the dangerous way of thinking now adopted by the Great Powers.

This early nineteenth-century cartoon illustrates Western fear of Russian expansion in the Balkans: Russia, the bear, is threatening Turkey. In the twentieth century internal unrest in the Balkans and the threat of Austria–Hungary, backed by Germany, became more of a concern.

Consider finally these words from the speech of Lloyd George, delivered in 1911 at the height of the second Moroccan crisis.

But if a situation were to be forced upon us in which peace could only be preserved . . . by allowing Britain to be treated . . . as if she were of no account in the Cabinet of Nations, then I say emphatically that peace at that price would be a humiliation intolerable for a great country like ours to endure.[21]

When people talk thus of war, perhaps the act itself is not far away.

The First Balkan War

When Britain and France signed the Entente Cordiale in 1904 they had agreed to settle their colonial disputes. Though not an alliance, it seemed a sensible way for two imperial powers to resolve their differences. Yet by the end of 1911 Britain found that the innocent-seeming Entente was helping to widen the dangerous gulf that had opened with Germany. Britain's fear of German colonial and naval plans (a third Navy Law had demanded an increase in the number of dreadnoughts by 1911) and the commercial rivalry between the two countries made relations sour enough. British support for France in two Moroccan crises led to this speech from a conservative German politician:

The Suez Canal, which formed the vital link between Britain and its colonies in the east. Any disturbance in the Balkans or the Middle East was seen by the British as a potential threat to the canal.

Now we know where our enemy stands. Like a flash of lightning in the night, these events have shown the German people where its enemy is. The German people now knows when it seeks its place in the sun . . . where the State is which thinks that it can decide the matter . . . When the hour of decision comes we are prepared for sacrifices, both of blood and of treasure.[22]

This speech shows the depth of Germany's

hostility toward Britain over the Moroccan crises and its willingness to go to war. Later the British Prime Minister, H. H. Asquith, was to write:

> *At the beginning of 1912 there was the strongest disposition in the British cabinet, which was, I believe, sincerely reciprocated [shared] by Herr von Bethmann [the German Chancellor], to settle outstanding disputes between the two countries.* [23]

But the British cabinet was being unrealistic in thinking it was still possible for Britain to keep its Entente with France and yet be friendly toward Germany. Lord Haldane visited Germany early in 1912 to try to reach an agreement, but he returned empty-handed. Later that year the First Balkan War made relations even more tense.

The cartoon below shows greedy powers tearing at the Balkans. Sir Edward Grey, the British Foreign Secretary, understood just why a Balkan war was dangerous:

> *Austria has determined that if Albania [the area on the coast below Montenegro] ceased to be Turkish territory it should not pass into the hands . . . of Serbia. Serbia, borne on the tide of her own victories, might easily reach the point of inevitable conflict with Austria. If this happened, and if Russia felt that she was required to support Serbia, European war was inevitable.* [24]

A Bulkan war affected the interests of the major powers and could easily lead to war.

German Imperial Army on battle maneuvers in 1909. As tension mounted, the major European powers increased their preparations for war. When the conflict finally came, cavalry were hardly used because they were so vulnerable to machine-gun fire.

A French cartoon from 1908. Franz Josef removes Bosnia–Herzegovina from the Turkish Empire while Franz Ferdinand declares Bulgaria's independence. Abdul Hamid looks on.

The Second Balkan War

The First Balkan War was concluded by a conference of ambassadors meeting in London from December 1912 to the summer of 1913. The problems faced by the negotiators were enormous. As an example, consider the question of the town of Scutari.

From the map below you can see that the fortified garrison town of Scutari held an important position, commanding the routes from the interior to the Adriatic coast. Throughout the First Balkan War it was held by the Turks. At the London peace conference these were the positions:

- The Turks were unwilling to surrender Scutari although it eventually fell in April 1913.
- Austria–Hungary wanted Scutari to go to the new state of Albania.
- Montenegro claimed Scutari for itself and finally took it in April.

- Serbia would have liked Scutari, to provide Serbia with access to the sea.

Austria–Hungary backed the new state of Albania. Russia supported the Slav state of Montenegro. It was difficult to resolve the issue. The key undoubtedly lay with Britain and Germany. Had they backed their respective partners, Montenegro and Austria–Hungary, then a major war might have broken out. But the German High Command told the country's politicians that they were not ready for war; and Grey also urged restraint on the Russians.

In the end, an international force took command of Scutari and awarded it to Albania.

The Second Balkan War broke out in June 1913. Bulgaria, feeling cheated by the London Conference of Ambassadors, attacked Serbia. Greece, Romania and Turkey then

By the end of the Balkan wars of 1912 and 1913 the Turkish Empire had been greatly reduced. Turkey's place in Europe was now taken by a dissatisfied complex of mutually suspicious Balkan states – a highly unstable situation.

States are colored as in 1878, with later acquisitions in lighter tints.
Ottoman boundary in 1900

Soldiers from Montenegro's army in 1913. By this date most Western armies had adopted camouflaged uniforms rather than the bright costumes the soldiers are seen wearing here.

joined forces with Serbia, hoping for gains for themselves. Bulgaria was crushed and had to surrender territory in order to secure a patched-up peace settlement at Bucharest on August 10.

Consider the situation in the Balkans at the end of 1913.

Britain had successfully negotiated a compromise, but had not backed Russia, its entente partner. If this were repeated in another crisis, perhaps the Germans might want to reach an agreement with Russia.

Austria–Hungary had seen Serbia and Montenegro expand, which was exactly what it had wanted to avoid.

Germany had urged its ally Austria–Hungary to restraint, but it would not be likely to do this again.

Russia, growing more powerful each day, was pledged to the cause of the independent Slav nations.

Serbia and Montenegro felt that they should have gained more from the wars.

Bulgaria had been humiliated and saw Austria as its natural ally against Serbia.

Turkey looked for revenge and reconquest.

The war had not resolved anything. Grey was justified when he wrote of the London Conference of Ambassadors, "We were sitting on a powder-magazine."[25]

Talk of war, 1914

It is tempting to view all international events before 1914 as steps toward war. In the last section, however, we saw Britain and Germany working to prevent the Balkans conflict from spreading, showing that two hostile powers could still work together. So was war bound to come?

The main difference in the European situation compared with that at the beginning of the century was that Britain was now no longer a strictly neutral power. Although its only major alliance was with Japan, Britain had ententes with France and Russia and had also formed military plans with them. For example, in 1912 the British agreed to leave protection of their interests in the Mediterranean to the French Navy, while the British fleet would defend the Channel. Yet the British were still wary of Russian plans in the Balkans, and had worked hard to limit Russian ambitions in the wars of 1912–13.

The French position had changed little since 1900. They were still implacably set against Germany, and their alliance with Russia had stood the test of time. In Morocco

A cartoon of "The Throne Perilous" from the British magazine *Punch*.

they had twice had the better of German ambitions. Talk of war was very much in the air. "The soldiers are of the opinion that it would be far better for France," wrote a British diplomat in 1913, "if a conflict were not too long postponed."[26]

Compare that remark with a statement by the Russia Foreign Minister, Sazonov, who claimed that the Triple Entente was growing stronger and stronger, and that "Germany was inevitably destined to come into conflict with this alliance."[27] It seems that Sazonov and the French soldiers felt that war was bound to come.

The cartoon of February 1914 on the facing page gives a British view of how the Italians (right) and Austro-Hungarians (left) viewed the new state of Albania. The "guards," Austria–Hungary and Italy, are inviting the new ruler of Albania onto his throne. But it is a "perilous throne" because both countries want to have control over Albania.

The third member of the Triple Alliance was Germany. Chief of the German General Staff, General Helmuth von Moltke, was anxious about the growth in power of the Triple Entente. "Today we would still be a match for them," he confided to the German Foreign Secretary. The diplomat continued:

In his opinion there was no alternative to making a preventive war in order to defeat the enemy while we still had a chance of victory. [He] . . . therefore proposed that I should conduct a policy with the aim of provoking a war in the near future.[28]

In this atmosphere of hostility, a world war was beginning to look inevitable.

▶ The Kaiser with his Chief of General Staff, Helmuth von Moltke. Von Moltke was made a scapegoat for the failure to capture Paris at the beginning of the war.

From Sarajevo to war 1914

IT IS EASY TO OVERSIMPLIFY steps by which the assassination at Sarajevo led to world war. In reality, the path to worldwide conflict was strewn with mistakes, misunderstandings and misjudgments. In outline this is what happened.

The death of Archduke Franz Ferdinand seemed to give Austria–Hungary a perfect excuse to destroy Serbia. The empire felt certain that Russia would not defend assassins. First, therefore, the imperial government in Vienna made sure that it had German support. This was guaranteed in early July, but the Austro-Hungarians then delayed: Austria called for immediate attack, Hungary for diplomatic moves. Not until July 23 was an ultimatum, deliberately intended to be unacceptable, sent to Serbia. By now memories of the assassination were fading. All eyes were on Serbia.

On July 24, the Russians, hoping to keep the conflict local, undertook limited military preparations. The very next day Serbia rejected the ultimatum and mobilized. On July 28, Austria declared war on Serbia and began shelling Belgrade. Montenegro sided with its large Slav neighbor. The Russians began full mobilization. In response, the Germans mobilized their forces on July 31, and demanded that Russia stop its preparations. When the Russians refused, Germany declared war on Russia on August 1.

With its ally Russia at war, France mobilized, and on August 3 Germany

The United States did not join World War I until April 1917 because for a long time it was seen as a European conflict that did not concern the U.S. Newspaper headlines from February 28, 1917 suggest that by then anxiety over the war was dominating the news.

INJURED INNOCENCE.

The German Ogre. "HEAVEN KNOWS THAT I HAD TO DO THIS IN SELF-DEFENCE; IT WAS FORCED UPON ME." (Aside) "FEE, FI, FO, FUM!"

[According to the Imperial Chancellor's latest utterance Germany is the deeply-wronged victim of British militarism.]

This cartoon of 1916 from *Punch* magazine offers the British explanation of why the war broke out, and who was to blame. It shows Germany as the aggressor.

declared war on France. Avoiding the main French defenses, the Germans moved into Belgium, planning to attack France from the north. Italy remained neutral, as did Britain until the Germans invaded Belgium.

In 1839, Britain and the other Great Powers had guaranteed the neutrality of Belgium by the Treaty of London. Britain now asked the Germans to withdraw. When they failed to do so, Britain declared war on Germany on August 4.

So far, although there was bound to be fighting at sea and in the overseas colonies, the conflict remained essentially European. Soon, however, it began to spread worldwide. Japan joined its British ally. The Turkish Empire joined Germany and Austria–

This fasinating photograph of Adolf Hitler was taken in Germany when war was declared in 1914. At first the war was very popular, but defeat brought ruin to Germany and this later enabled Hitler to come to power.

Hungary later in 1914, as did Bulgaria in 1915 when Serbia's fate seemed sealed.

Italy did not join the war until 1915, but when it did it took sides with the Anglo-French allies, lured by promises of territory around the Adriatic. Romania and Portugal followed suit in 1916, and Greece and the United States in 1917. The United States remained neutral until German submarine attacks on its Atlantic shipping stung it into action. When this happened there was truly a world war.

The ultimatum

At 7:35 p.m. on July 5, 1914, Count Szögyeny, the Austro-Hungarian ambassador in Berlin, sent this telegram to his Foreign Minister, Count Berchtold:

> After lunch, when I again called attention to the seriousness of the situation, the Kaiser authorized me to inform our gracious Majesty [the Austro-Hungarian Emperor] that we might in this case, as in all others, rely upon Germany's full support . . . he did not doubt in the least that Herr von Bethmann-Hollweg would agree with him . . . But it was his [Kaiser William's] opinion that this action must not be delayed. Russia's attitude will no doubt be hostile, but . . . Russia at the present time was in no way prepared for war.[29]

This telegram gives the impression that the Kaiser was preparing for war. It continues, "Kaiser William intends leaving tomorrow morning for Kiel, whence he starts for his northern tour." This "tour" was a summer cruise.

Armed with this promise of German support, but ignoring the Kaiser's advice to move fast, the Austro-Hungarians drew up their ultimatum. It stated flatly, without proof, that "the murder at Sarajevo was prepared in Belgrade [the capital of Serbia]." In the light of this, it went on to make ten harsh demands on Serbia. For example, according to the third clause the Serbian government had:

> . . . to eliminate without delay from public instruction everything that serves or might serve the propaganda against Austria–Hungary, both where teachers or books are concerned.

Considering the universal hatred and fear of Austria–Hungary in Serbia, this would have had a devastating effect on the country's education system.

Perhaps the fourth clause, however, was the most humiliating.

> . . . to remove from military service and from the administration all officers and officials who are guilty of having taken part in the propaganda against Austria–Hungary, whose names and proofs of whose guilt the Imp [erial] and Royal Government [of Austria–Hungary] will communicate to the Royal Government of Serbia.[30]

Franz Josef (1830-1916), Emperor of Austria and King of Hungary at the outbreak of World War I. His government waited until they felt that they could rely on German support before issuing their unacceptable ultimatum to Serbia.

Serbia could not accept such clauses, although its reply to the ultimatum was reasonable and moderate.

The cartoon on the facing page shows how *Punch* magazine saw the situation. The three

Punch **cartoon from July 29, 1914.**

THE POWER BEHIND.

animals represent Austria–Hungary, Serbia and Russia. But the cartoon does not show Germany backing Austria and France backing Russia. In 1908, when Austria–Hungary had annexed Bosnia and Herzegovina, France had not stood by its Russian ally. Now, in July 1914, the French ambassador in St.Petersburg said:

> *France would not only give Russia strong diplomatic support but would, if necessary, fulfill all the obligations imposed on her by the alliance.* [31]

The Great Powers were clearly less restrained than they had been in previous crises.

The Schlieffen Plan

Neither the French nor the Russians had welcomed the emergence of the German Empire. The new power was seen as a threat. Bismarck, the great German statesman and Chancellor, realized this and used his diplomatic skill to prevent an alliance between France and Russia. But even before Bismarck was dismissed in 1890, the German military had prepared plans to fight a defensive war on two fronts.

Count Alfred von Schlieffen, Chief of the German General Staff from 1891 to 1905, was responsible for an offensive German war strategy and a plan that was to form the basis of the German attack in 1914.

Germany must strive . . . first to strike down one of the allies while the other is kept occupied; but then, when the one antagonist is conquered, it must, by exploiting its railroads, bring a superiority of numbers to the other theater of war, which will also destroy the other enemy . . .[32]

From 1892 onward this meant for Germany a quick, decisive blow against France through Belgium, before switching all forces against Russia. Schlieffen and his successor, General von Moltke, believed that the

... marque d'infamie, devrait se porter au front, comme la fleur de lys à l'épaule du forçat.
Dessin de A. Robida.

A French cartoon of the Kaiser with his leading Generals, 1915. The Germans believed that since war was bound to come, they should strike first to avoid having to fight on two fronts. This picture suggests what the French thought of such action.

Austro-Hungarian forces could keep Russia occupied while the Germans dealt with France. The map below shows both von Schlieffen's original plan and von Moltke's revised plan. Von Moltke wished to avoid going through the Netherlands to attack France.

Consider the effect in July 1914 of Germany's being tied to the Schlieffen plan, as adapted by von Moltke. On July 30, full Russian mobilization was ordered. The confrontation was between Russia and Austria–Hungary over Serbia, with Germany backing Austria–Hungary. The Kaiser had asked why not limit the war and attack only Russia? "I assured His Majesty that this was not possible," von Moltke wrote.

The deployment of an army of a million men was not a matter of improvization. It was the product of a whole heavy year's work and once worked out, could not be changed.[33]

The Schlieffen Plan, in fact, served to extend the conflict.

Moreover, if there was to be a war then the Germans had to strike first for their plan to work.

In other words: the gamble of the Schlieffen Plan was so great that it could only succeed as a result of a rapid surprise advance of the Germans or by a sudden onslaught on Belgium. In the opinion of the General Staff, Germany was therefore obliged by purely technical necessities to adopt, before the whole world, the role of a brutal aggressor.[34]

It could be argued, therefore, that the Schlieffen Plan turned a Balkan conflict into

A comparison of the Von Schlieffen Plan and the Von Moltke Plan shows how they differed subtly, but significantly.

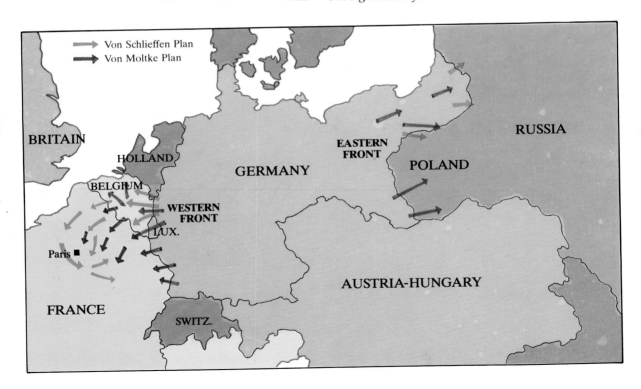

A scrap of paper

In *The War That Will End War*, published in 1914, H. G. Wells sets out the reasons why he thought Britain had gone to war:

> *The cause of this war was the invasion of Luxembourg and Belgium. We declared war because we were bound by treaty to declare war. We have been pledged to protect the integrity of Belgium since the kingdom of Belgium has existed. If the Germans had not broken the guarantees they shared with us to respect the neutrality of these little States we should certainly not be at war at the present time.*[35]

H. G. Wells is arguing here that Britain went to war as a matter of high principle.

Consider the famous *Punch* cartoon opposite of August 1914. Brave little Belgium is blocking the path of the German bully. This reflected the idealistic attitude in Britain at the time. The German Chancellor Berthmann-Hollweg called the 1839 Treaty of London that guaranteed Belgian neutrality a "scrap of paper." He did not believe that Britain would go to war over it; yet, according to H. G. Wells and this cartoon, the Chancellor was wrong. But there is another point of view.

On July 29, the British cabinet discussed the European situation, including what to do if the Germans invaded Belgium; they "decided not to decide."[36] The cabinet felt that the duty of protecting Belgium's neutrality was not just Britain's, but that of all the powers who had signed the 1839 Treaty. Perhaps, when Britain did declare war, Belgium was just a popular excuse.

The Foreign Office knew why Britain should go to war:

> *The argument that there is no written bond binding us to France is strictly correct . . . But the Entente has been made, strengthened, put to the test and celebrated in a manner justifying the belief that a moral bond was being forged . . . our duty and our interest will be seen to be in standing by France.*[37]

Sir Edward Grey felt the same (although to the House of Commons he also emphasized the duty toward Belgium):

> *We felt that to stand aside would mean the domination of Germany; the subordination of France and Russia; the isolation of Britain . . . and ultimately that Germany would wield the whole power of the Continent. How would she use it as regards Britain?*[38]

On the other hand, one modern historian has written that "Britain's entry into the war had little to do with Belgium."[39]

◀ German 1914 cartoon of Grey as a shopkeeper, selling death.
▶ *Punch* cartoon reflecting British public opinion of the outbreak of war.

BRAVO. BELGIUM!

World War

HE WONT BE HAPPY TILL HE GETS IT

EUROPE

A British postcard of 1914, showing the Kaiser as a spoiled child in the bathtub wanting Europe all to himself. But William II was not entirely to blame for the outbreak of World War I.

The previous pages have suggested that the Great Powers went to war not to fulfill their treaty obligations, but because their vital interests were threatened. A further example of how a nation put its own needs before its treaty promises was demonstrated by Italy.

In July 1914 the Italian Prime Minister wrote to the King of Italy that the government had:

> . . . up to the present said and done nothing that might limit Italy's freedom of action . . . We are . . . convinced that it is most difficult, perhaps impossible, and certainly extremely dangerous to drag Italy into taking part in an eventual war provoked by Austria and waged in the interest of Austria.[40]

In the end secret promises lured Italy into the war. Sir Edward Grey recalled the negotiations of 1915:

> If Italy was to take the risk of war, she must know where she would be at the end of it. Her claims might overlap the aspirations of Serbia, or even Greece. We did not want to dishearten Serbia in her uphill struggle with Austria, nor to alienate Greece by an agreement with Italy that might be regarded as made at the expense of the legitimate aspirations [lawful ambitions] of either of the two smaller countries . . . There were difficulties and delays, but it was essential to the Allies that the negotiations should succeed; the conditions were agreed, and Italy entered the war against Austria.[41]

A glance at the map on page 34 will show clearly how Italy's interests could easily conflict with those of Serbia, Greece and even Russia.

The same spirit of national interest coming before principle can be detected in these extracts from speeches by President Woodrow Wilson of the United States. The first was made in 1914, as he urged his country to neutrality. The second was delivered to Congress in 1917, asking it to declare war:

1 *The effect of the war upon the United States will depend upon what American citizens say and do. Every man who really loves America will act and speak in the true spirit of neutrality . . . The United States must be neutral in fact as well as in name . . .*

2 *The present German submarine warfare against commerce is a warfare against mankind.*

It is a war against all nations. American ships have been sunk, American lives taken, in ways which it has stirred us very deeply to learn of . . .

With a profound sense of the solemn and even tragical character of the step I am taking . . . I advise that the Congress declare the recent course of the Imperial German Government to be in fact nothing less than war against the government and people of the United States.[42]

A street scene in New York outside a draft post, where all ablebodied young men were required to sign on for military service.

Can anyone be blamed?

THE TREATY OF VERSAILLES was the settlement made at the end of World War I. It was drawn up by the victorious allies: the United States, France and Britain. The defeated nations were not asked to the negotiations, but had to sign the Treaty. Clause 231 made it quite clear whom the Allies held responsible for the war:

The Allied and Associated Governments affirm and Germany accepts the responsibility of Germany and her allies for causing the loss and damage to which the Allied and Associated Governments and their nationals have been subjected as a consequence of the war imposed upon them by the aggression of Germany and her allies.[43]

French sailors in action in Morocco in 1907. Although world war did not break out until 1914, incidents such as the one pictured above could easily have sparked a war had they been handled differently.

The Treaty was only putting into words feelings widely expressed in 1914 and throughout the war. But can Germany really be blamed? The views of historians have changed.

1 Between the First and Second World Wars, German and Allied scholars took opposing views. Some Germans held that no one power was to blame. They emphasized the network of alliances, the arms race, and commercial and colonial rivalry, all of which made war likely. They then cited the spark of the Sarajevo assassination, which set in motion a string of events, like falling dominoes, that could not be stopped. Other German scholars maintained that Germany was forced, by British imperialism and Russian military expansion, to fight a "preventive" war. In other words, what appeared an offensive was in fact a defensive war. Even historians from

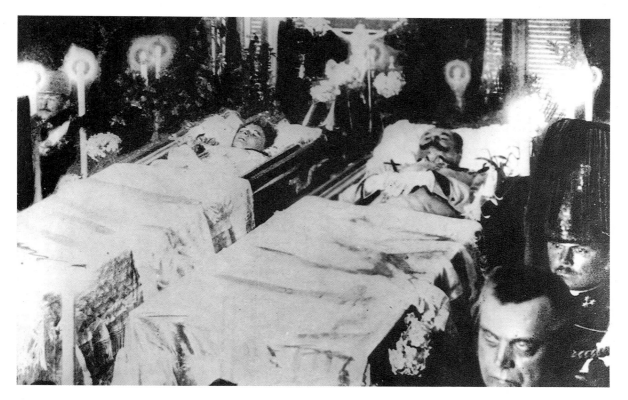

Archduke Franz Ferdinand and his wife, Sophie, lying in state after their assassination at Sarajevo, 1914. If the Archduke had listened to advice and not made the risky trip to Bosnia when he did, then the course of history may have been different. Or perhaps war was inevitable.

the victorious nations thought it was too simple to blame only Germany. They found evidence to suggest that all governments concerned had made mistakes and behaved aggressively at times.

2 The Second World War, everyone agreed, was caused by the aggression of Hitler's Nazi Germany. But by the 1950s most historians had come to the view that it was not correct to blame the Germans for the outbreak of the First World War as well. There was after all, they felt, much truth in the view that Europe was collectively responsible.

3 In 1961 the German historian Fritz Fischer published an influential book in which he concluded that the German ruling class, whether under the Kaiser or under Hitler, consistently sought to dominate Europe. So once more Germany was blamed for the outbreak of the Great War, and many

scholars, both outside Germany and within, have accepted this view.

4 Today we are more concerned with why events, such as wars, happen than with who is to blame. The Sarajevo crisis was not very different from many other crises that occurred between 1900 and 1914, except that this time no side would back down. When the Russians mobilized to protect Serbia, the Germans had two choices: either to stand by Austria–Hungary or to accept diplomatic defeat and humiliation. They chose the former course, and so a local war became a European and finally a world war. Germany can hardly be blamed for failing to foresee the outcome.

How far back?

In order to understand why things happen, historians often divide causes into "long term" and "short term." The long-term causes form the background that makes an event likely to happen; the short-term causes provide an explanation of why events happened as they did. In the case of World War I the immediate, or short-term, causes are usually seen as the assassination at Sarajevo and the events immediately fol-lowing it. But those events cannot be understood without a knowledge of their background. Here are three examples:

- It is not possible to understand why Russia stood so resolutely behind Serbia in 1914 without knowing how Serbian interests had been thwarted at the end of the two Balkan wars of 1912–13; or without knowing how Russia had been humiliated when Austria–Hungary took

This *Punch* cartoon shows Bismarck as a puppet master controlling the Emperors of Germany, Austria and Russia. The origins of the war of 1914 can be traced back at least to the time of Bismarck.

THE THREE EMPERORS;

OR, THE VENTRILOQUIST OF VARZIN!

Napoleon at Eylau. The Europe that went to war in 1914 was in many ways the Europe created after the fall of Napoleon I. Some would argue, therefore, that an examination of the outbreak of the World War I should start with Napoleonic Europe.

Archduke Franz Ferdinand and his wife just before their assassination at Sarajevo. One cannot understand why their deaths sparked off a train of events that led to world war unless one studies the years preceding the murder.

over Bosnia and Herzegovina in 1908.

- We cannot understand France's hatred of Germany without knowledge of the Franco-Prussian War of 1870–71, when Germany was awarded the rich province of Alsace and half of Lorraine.
- Britain's fear that a single large power might dominate the continent, as Germany seemed to want to do in 1914, cannot be properly grasped without reference to Napoleon I or even Louis XIV. When both these powerful rulers, the former in the early nineteenth century and the latter in the early eighteenth century, looked as if they were going to gain control over most of Europe, Britain doggedly opposed them. In particular, Britain feared lest the Low Countries (the

Netherlands and Belgium) should fall into the hands of an enemy. The ports of the Low Countries were ideal jumping-off points for an invasion of Britain.

These attempts to understand the long-term causes of World War I has taken us back to the reign of Louis XIV (1643–1715)! It is difficult to know where to start when trying to unravel the causes.

One theory is that when Britain became involved in the European alliance system, the pattern of the forces of 1914 was more or less settled. Other historians go back to Bismarck's dismissal in 1890, the Franco-Prussian War, or the establishment of the nineteenth-century state system at the Congress of Vienna in 1815. Wherever it starts, the story will be incomplete.

The causes

Any explanation of the long-term causes of the First World War must include the following points:

- The rise of nationalism in Europe gave peoples such as the Serbs great pride in their country, inspiring nationalists like Gavrilo Princip.
- The alliance system, which divided the continent into "armed camps," made it more likely that an incident could not be prevented from spreading.
- The arms race frightened the politicians; they had to demand higher and higher taxes to pay for more weapons, because they dared not fall behind rival powers in military strength.
- The naval arms race between Britain and Germany bred mistrust between them.
- Commercial rivalry led to greater hostility between the major industrial nations.
- Colonial or imperial rivalry meant that European powers were likely to have conflicting interests in different parts of the world, as France and Germany did over Morocco.
- The existence of the Schlieffen Plan meant that German mobilization could not stop once it had started; it also made it imperative for Germany to strike first.
- The proud group of militarists within Germany, calling for a world role for their country, worried other powers and put pressure on the government for aggressive action.

To these factors must be added the effect on countries that faced humiliation, as for

Nationalism is often held up as a cause of World War I. Strong national feeling is illustrated in this 1907 picture of a Russian who had fired at French soldiers from a bus in Paris being set upon by the other passengers.

A German picture of a U-boat in action. As the two armed camps in Europe built up their armaments, so the temptation to use them became greater.

example when:
- Germany failed to prevent French domination of Morocco in 1905–06 and 1911.
- Russia had to watch Austria–Hungary absorb Bosnia and Herzegovina in 1908.
- Serbia was prevented from gaining access to the Adriatic coast in 1913.

Armed conflict was inevitable the next time each one of these countries was forced into a corner.

Moreover, many mistakes were made. For example:
- Did the Kaiser realize what he was doing when he gave Austria–Hungary a "blank check" of support in July 1914?
- Did the Russians realize what might happen when they mobilized on July 28–31, 1914?

Finally, chance played its part:
- What might have happened, for example, if the Archduke's car had not taken the wrong turning on June 28, 1914?

The war was not inevitable: different actions by any of the powers concerned might have altered the chain of events. When German Chancellor Bethmann-Hollweg was later asked why war broke out, he replied with a sigh, "Oh – if I only knew!"[44]

Leading figures

Asquith, Herbert Henry (1852–1928) British Prime Minister 1908–16

A Liberal, Asquith believed in peaceful policies wherever possible, but almost against his will found his government increasingly drawn into international affairs and the arms race. He was Prime Minister during the crises in 1908 over Bosnia–Herzegovina and in 1911 over Morocco and during the two Balkan wars. In the end he and his Foreign Secretary, Sir Edward Grey, believed that Britain had to side with France when war broke out in 1914. Reluctantly, most of his cabinet came to agree with his point of view.

Berchtold, Count Leopold (1863–1942) Austro-Hungarian diplomat

After serving in Paris and London, in 1906 Berchtold succeeded Aehrenthal as the Austro-Hungarian ambassador to Russia in St. Petersburg. Six years later, he again succeeded Aehrenthal, this time to the post of Foreign Minister, which he held until 1915. Encouraged by Conrad, the Austro-Hungarian Chief of General Staff, Berchtold did what he could to prevent the expansion of Serbia and other Slav states. This inevitably brought his country more into conflict with Russia. In 1913 Berchtold prevented Serbia from gaining access to the Adriatic Sea and in 1914, following the assassination of Archduke Franz Ferdinand, Berchtold was largely responsible for the severe ultimatum given to Serbia. He had not involved Italy, his partner in the Triple Alliance, in his strategy.

Fisher, John (1841–1920) British Admiral

After three years as Commander-in-Chief in the Mediterranean, in 1904 Admiral Fisher became Britain's First Sea Lord. This gave him control over naval policy. For the next six years he was responsible for the construction of the dreadnought battleships and the almost complete reorganization of the British Navy. Fisher was worried by the expansion of the German Navy and he redrew Britain's naval plans, considering Germany the prime enemy. Ironically, the effect of this was to inspire the Germans to build up their navy and so a naval arms race began. Fisher had four years out of office before returning as First Sea Lord on the outbreak of war in 1914.

Franz Josef (1830–1916) Emperor of Austria–Hungary

After a fiercely strict upbringing, Franz Josef became Emperor of Austria in 1848. In 1867 he was crowned King of Hungary: his empire became the Dual Monarchy of Austria–Hungary. Under the influence of his early years, the Emperor rigidly put the needs of his empire before all else. Having signed the Dual Alliance with Germany in 1879 he would not be diverted from this policy. Urged on by militarist advisers such as Conrad, his Chief of Staff, he authorized the ultimatum to Serbia in July 1914. Thus he led his empire into a war, the scope and consequences of which he did not have the intelligence or imagination to foresee.

Grey, Sir Edward (1862–1933) British Foreign Secretary 1905–16

Sir Edward Grey played a major part in all European events leading to the outbreak of war in 1914. A Liberal, Grey believed firmly in trying to avoid war, but when it came he reluctantly reached the conclusion that Britain's interests could be served only by actively siding with France and Russia. In 1907 he had overseen the forming of the Entente with Russia, although he later opposed Russian ambition in the Balkans in 1908 and 1913. He stood strongly by France in the second Moroccan crisis (1911) but the next year tried once more to come to an understanding with Germany over the naval arms race. At the time of the two Balkan wars (1912–13) Grey worked hard and successfully to negotiate a peaceful settlement for the area, but the results of his efforts were short-lived.

Izvolsky, Alexander (1856–1919) Russian Foreign Minister 1906–10

Izvolsky became Russia's Foreign Minister in 1906. His greatest achievement was the Entente negotiated with Britain in 1907. The following year, however, he was deceived by the Austro-Hungarian Foreign Minister, Aehrenthal, into sanctioning Austria–Hungary's annexation of Bosnia and Herzegovina. When Russia proposed the passage of its warships from the Black Sea through the Dardanelles into the eastern Mediterranean (as Aehrenthal had suggested) the other European powers would not support the idea. Russia's relations with Austria–Hungary were irrecoverably damaged. In 1910 Izvolsky became Russian ambassador in Paris. Germans were later to accuse him of planning to isolate Germany by surrounding the country with hostile alliances.

Moltke, Helmuth von (1848–1916) German General

Von Moltke was the nephew of the more famous "elder Moltke" (1800–91), who masterminded Prussia's remarkable victories over Austria (1866) and France (1870–71). Moltke "the Younger" became Chief of the German General Staff in 1905, although he did not believe in his ability to do the job. He altered, and weakened, the famous Schlieffen Plan for an attack on France before Russia, and did not wholeheartedly support the more aggressive of the Kaiser's advisers who called for a war sooner rather than later. In the crises before the war, and when the fighting began, von Moltke was too hesitant to be effective. He was a cultured man, happier playing the cello than planning for war.

Tirpitz, Alfred von (1849–1930) German Admiral

Admiral Tirpitz was appointed German Minister of Marine in 1897. At once he set about creating a large new German navy, powerful enough to defend Germany's overseas trade and colonies. This at once brought suspicion and hostility from Britain, which considered itself the unquestioned world supreme naval power. When Britain built dreadnought battleships, Tirpitz made sure that Germany did the same – thus escalating a naval arms race. Tirpitz organized a German Navy League to propagate his views in Germany. He resigned in 1916 when the Kaiser would not allow him to use the navy as aggressively as he wished.

William II, Kaiser (1859–1941) Emperor of Germany 1888–1918

Throughout his life William (who had a physical disability in the form of a "withered" arm) felt inferior to some of the other rulers of Europe, particularly those from Britain. He longed for glory and success. When he came to the throne he urged his country away from the moderate policies of Bismarck (whom he dismissed in 1890) toward a more aggressive world role. He encouraged the construction of a large navy and massive armies, trying to make sure that Germany would be the undisputed leader of Europe. Although perhaps he did not seek war, his tactless comments led the other European powers into believing that he did. After a brief illness in 1908 he was never again fully in charge of affairs in Germany, although he had come to believe in the need for a "preventive" war by 1914. He may not have realized that war would come about when he promised support to Austria–Hungary in the early days of July 1914.

Important Dates

Date	
1815	Final defeat of Napoleon I (Bonaparte) at Waterloo.
	Congress of Vienna settles peace terms: German Confederation established.
1819	German Customs Union (*Zollverein*) begins, in effect until 1867.
1830	Greece declared independent from Turkish Empire.
1839	By Treaty of London the major powers guarantee Belgian neutrality.
1848	Revolution widespread in Europe.
1852	Napoleon III confirmed Emperor of France.
1853	Russo-Turkish War.
1854–56	Crimean War, ending with Treaty of Paris.
1859–61	Except for Venice (1866) and Rome (1870), Italy united under King Victor Emmanuel II.
1861	Romania formed and is fully independent by 1877.
1866	Prussia defeats Austria in Seven Weeks' War.
1867	Austrian Empire becomes Austro-Hungarian Dual Monarchy.
1870–71	Franco-Prussian War; France defeated; Alsace and much of Lorraine ceded to German Empire *May 1871.*
1871	*January* German Empire proclaimed with William I as Emperor and Bismarck as Chancellor.
1872	Emperors of Germany, Russia and Austria form the Alliance of the Three Emperors.
1877–78	Russo-Turkish War.
1878	Powers mediate terms between Russia and Turkey at Congress of Berlin.
1879	Germany introduces protectionist tariff policies.
	Austro-German Dual Alliance.
1881	Alliance of the Three Emperors renewed (see 1872).
1882	Germany, Austria and Italy form Triple Alliance.
1884–85	Berlin Conference on Africa: Germany acquires African colonies.
1884	Alliance of the Three Emperors renewed.
1885	Britain and Russia clash over Afghanistan.
1887	Alliance of the Three Emperors expires.
	Reinsurance Treaty between Germany and Russia.
	Mediterranean Agreement between Britain, Austria–Hungary, Spain and Italy.
	Triple Alliance renewed.
1888	William II becomes Emperor of Germany.
1890	*March* Bismarck dismissed.
	June Reinsurance Treaty not renewed.
	Germany takes possession of Tanganyika (now part of Tanzania).
1891	Franco-Russian political understanding signed.
	Triple Alliance (see 1887) renewed until 1902.
1892	Franco-Russian military convention concluded.
1894	Franco-Russian alliance ratified.
1896	"Kruger Telegram" from William II to Boer leader.
1897	Austro-Russian agreement on Balkans.
	Germans seize Kiaochow Bay from China.
1898	Franco-British tension at Fashoda on the upper Nile.
	First German Navy Law.
1899–1902	Boer War in South Africa.
1900	Second German Navy Law announces German Navy to double to 38 first-class battleships by 1920.
	Russia occupies Manchuria.
1902	Secret Franco-Italian treaty.
	Triple Alliance (see 1891) renewed until 1913.
	Anglo-Japanese alliance.
1903	Mürzsteg agreement between Russia and Austria–Hungary.
1904	Anglo-French Entente Cordiale.
1904–05	Russo-Japanese War.
1905	Schlieffen Plan finalized; German offensive against France to pass through Belgium.
	First Moroccan crisis.
	Treaty of Björkö between William II and Nicholas II of Russia.
	Revolution in Russia.

1906	*Jan–April* Algeciras Conference settles Moroccan question.
	HMS *Dreadnought* launched.
	New German Navy Law: Dreadnought-type battleships adopted and Kiel Canal to be widened to accommodate them.
1907	Britain establishes British Expeditionary Force, with Territorial Army for home defense.
	Anglo-Russian Entente; Triple Entente established.
1908	*September* Izvolsky and Aehrenthal make Buchlau agreement.
	October Austria–Hungary annexes Bosnia and Herzegovina. The other powers object to Russian proposal to open the Straits of the Bosphorous and Dardanelles to Russian warships.
1911	Second Moroccan crisis.
	July Lloyd-George's Mansion House speech regarded as a warning to Germany.
	October Italo-Turkish War (to October 1912).
1912	*February* Lord Haldane visits Berlin.
	May Greece, Serbia, Montenegro and Bulgaria form Balkan League.
	July Franco-British Naval Agreement.
	October First Balkan War (to 1913): Balkan League defeats Turkey.
1913	*May* Treaty of London ends Balkan War.
	June Turkey, Serbia, Greece and Romania defeat Bulgaria in Second Balkan War (to Treaty of Bucharest, *August*).
	November German officer appointed Inspector-General of Turkish Army.
1914	*June 28* Archduke Franz Ferdinand assassinated at Sarajevo.
	July 23 Austro-Hungarian ultimatum to Serbia.
	July 25 Serbia's reply rejected by Austria–Hungary.
	July 28 Austria–Hungary declares war on Serbia.
	Russia begins to mobilize.
	July 31 German ultimatum to Russia.
	August 1 Germany mobilizes and declares war on Russia.
	France mobilizes.
	August 2 Germany gives ultimatum to Belgium and sends troops into Luxembourg.
	August 3 Germany declares war on France.
	August 4 Britain gives ultimatum to Germany.
	Britain declares war on Germany, on expiration of ultimatum at midnight.
	August 12 Britain and France declare war on Austria–Hungary.
	August 23 Japan joins Allies.
	November Turkey joins Central Powers.
1915	*May* Italy joins war on Allied side.
	October Bulgaria joins Central Powers.
1917	*April* United States declares war on Germany.

Glossary

Absolute power	Unlimited power to rule, with no constitutional limits.
Alliance	A bond or treaty made between countries to further their common interests.
Ally	A state linked to another by treaty or league.
Ambassador	An official envoy from one state to another.
Annex	To take over territory by conquest or occupation.
Antagonism	Hostility or opposition.
Archduke	A prince of the Austrian royal family.
Assassinate	To murder an important public figure, often for political reasons.
Autobiography	A person's own life story.
Balkans	The territory on the peninsula between the Black Sea and the Adriatic Sea.
Black Hand	A Serbian secret society that used terrorist methods with the goal of liberating Serbs outside Serbia from Hapsburg rule.
Cabinet	Group of senior, policy-making ministers of a government.
Capital	Money used for investment.
Chancellor	The German chief minister.
Civil servant	Member of the administrative service of a government.
Coalition	A government made up of more than one political party.
Colony	Overseas territory administered by another country.
Commercial	Relating to economic needs.
Compromise	To settle a dispute by finding a solution that satisfies all sides.
Continent, the	Europe, excluding the off-shore islands.
Crisis	A situation of extreme danger.
Czar	The hereditary emperor of Russia; from the Latin "Caesar."
Dardanelles	The southern end of the sea passage from the Black Sea to the Mediterranean Sea.
Democracy	Rule by the people or their elected representatives.
Deployment	Setting out, arranging.
Despotism	Government by a single ruler with absolute power.
Diplomat	A skilled negotiator, especially in international relations.
Economy	A country's finances, trade and industry.
Emancipate	To set free.
Empire	Widespread territories and peoples under one government.
Entente	An understanding between nations.
Foreign Secretary	Government minister in charge of foreign affairs.
Free trade	International trade based on exchange of goods without customs duties.
Front	The line of battle nearest the enemy.
Garrison	Troops stationed on a military base.
Imperialism	Policy of making or maintaining an empire.
Inevitable	Unavoidable, certain to happen.
Isolation	Being cut off; policy of avoiding political links with other countries.
Kaiser	German word meaning "Emperor," from the Latin "Caesar."
Maritime	Relating to the sea and shipping.
Militarism	Dominance of a military viewpoint; policy of aggressive military preparedness for action.

Minister	Government officer.
Mobilize	To make armed forces ready for war.
Nationalism	Feeling of patriotism and desire to make one's country strong and independent.
Nazi	Member of the National Socialist German Workers' Party, which seized power in Germany under Adolf Hitler.
Negotiate	Attempt to settle a matter by discussion.
Neutral	Not taking sides.
Obsolete	Out of date.
Orthodox Church	The Russian or Greek Christian Church, called the Eastern Orthodox Church.
Press, the	Newspapers and magazines.
Propaganda	The systematic spreading of ideas and opinions with the aim of converting others, or bringing about change.
Protectionism	Helping domestic industry by taxing imports.
Reparations	Compensation in money or materials paid by a defeated country to the victor.
Republic	A state in which the citizens hold supreme power.
Resolve	To settle. To find the solution for a problem.
Slav	Member of any of the peoples of eastern Europe or Soviet Asia.
Sphere of interest	Area in which a country claims to have the major influence.
Statesman	An influential and internationally respected politician.
Stock exchange	A place where stocks and bonds are bought and sold.
Strait	Narrow channel of water linking two areas of sea.
Strategy	Overall plan of campaign.
Tariff	Tax on goods entering or leaving a country.
Terrorist	One who uses terror to further his or her political ends.
Treaty	A written agreement between nations.
Turbine	A high-powered rotary engine, introduced in the late nineteenth century.
Ultimatum	A final demand.
Unification	The creation of one country out of a number of smaller states.
Violate	To encroach, to break an agreement.
Zollverein	The customs union of German states organized in the early 1819.

Picture acknowledgments

The author and publisher would like to thank the following for allowing their illustrations to be reproduced in this book: Aldus Archive 15 (left), 38 (left), 47; E.T. Archive 4, 10, 16, 31; Imperial War Museum 33 (left); Mansell Collection 17 (bottom), 19, 25 (bottom), 37, 49; Mary Evans Picture Library cover, 6, 7, 8, 9 (top & bottom), 11 (right), 13, 18, 21, 22 (right), 23, 26, 27 (top), 32, 33 (right), 35, 39, 44, 48, 50, 52, 53; Punch 12, 29 (top), 36, 38 (right), 41, 45; Topham Picture Library 7, 11 (left), 15 (right), 20, 22 (left), 25 (top), 29 (bottom), 30, 40, 42, 46, 51 (right); Wayland Picture Library 5, 17 (top), 27 (bottom), 51 (left). The maps were supplied by Malcolm Walker.

Further reading

Text Books

Albertini, Luigi. *The Origins of the War of Nineteen Hundred Fourteen*, 3 vols. Massey, Isabella trans. Greenwood, 1980

Barnett, Correlli. *The Swordbearers*, Indiana Univ. Press, 1975

Beard, Charles A. *Devil Theory of War: An Inquiry into the Nature of History*, Greenwood, 1968

Churchill, Winston S. *World Crisis, 1911–18*, 2 vols. New Amercian Library, 1968

Luxembourg, Rosa. *The Crisis in German Social Democracy, 1918*, Fertig

Schmitt, Bernadotte E. *The Coming of the War, 1914*, 2 vols. Fertig, 1968

Turner, L. C. *Origins of the First World War*, Norton, 1970

Notes on sources

1 Boyd, C. W. (ed.), *Mr Chamberlain's Speeches*, Constable, 1914, volume 2, p. 142.
2 Cited in Geiss, Imanuel (ed.), *July 1914 The Outbreak of the First World War: Selected Documents*, Batsford, 1967, p. 23.
3 Cited in Albertini, Luigi, *The Origins of the War of 1914*, translated by Massey, Isabella M., Oxford, 1952, volume 1, p. 103.
4 Grey, Viscount, *Twenty-Five Years 1892–1916*, Hodder and Stoughton, 1925, volume 2, p. 52.
5 Martin, Gilbert, *Recent History Atlas*, Weidenfeld and Nicolson, 1966.
6 Asquith, H. H., *The Genesis of the War*, Cassell, 1923, p. 75.
7 A memorandum to the Navy Law of 1900, cited in *ibid.*, p. 71.
8 Asquith, *op. cit.*, p. 20.
9 *Ibid.*, p. 23.
10 Albertini, *op. cit.*, volume 1, p. 146.
11 Mantel, Gordon, *The Origins of the First World War*, Longman, 1987, p. 46.
12 Cited in Albertini, *op. cit.*, volume I, pp. 150–151.
13 *Ibid.*, p. 149.
14 Grey, *op. cit.*, volume 1, p. 113.
15 *Ibid.*, pp. 152–3.
16 *Ibid.*, p. 154.
17 Sazonov, S., *Fateful Years, 1909–1916*, Cape, 1928, p. 30.
18 Cited in Albertini, *op. cit.*, volume 1, p. 189.
19 Cited in Parkinson, *op. cit.*, pp. 60–61.
20 Sazonov, *op. cit.*, pp. 49–51.
21 Cited in Asquith, *op. cit.*, p. 93.
22 Cited in Albertini, *op. cit.*, volume 1, p. 334.
23 Asquith, *op. cit.*, p. 97.
24 Grey, *op. cit.*, volume 1, p. 264.
25 *Ibid.*, p. 268.
26 Cited in Albertini, *op. cit.*, volume 1, p. 424.
27 Sazonov, *op. cit.*, p. 128.
28 Cited in Röhl, John (ed.), *1914: Delusion or Design?*, Elek, 1973, p. 32.
29 Cited in Geiss, Imanuel (ed.), *July 1914*, Deutscher Taschenbuch Verlag, Munich, 1967, pp. 76–77.
30 *Ibid.*, pp. 43, 145.
31 As reported by the British ambassador, cited in Albertini, *op. cit.*, volume 2, p. 295.
32 Cited in Parkinson, *op. cit.*, p. 79.
33 *Ibid.*, p. 84.
34 Ritter, G., cited in "The Significance of the Schlieffen Plan" by Turner, L.C.F., in Kennedy, Paul (ed.), *The War Plans of the Great Powers, 1880–1914*, Allen and Unwin, 1979, p. 216.
35 *Ibid.*, p. 7.
36 Cited in Steiner, *op. cit.*, p. 224.
37 *Ibid.*, p. 228.
38 Grey, *op. cit.*, volume 1, p. 337.
39 Mantel, *op. cit.*, p. 69.
40 Cited in Albertini, *op. cit.*, volume 2, p. 318.
41 Grey, *op. cit.*, volume 2, p. 208.
42 Both extracts from Hofstadter, Richard (ed.), *Great Issues in American History*, 2 volumes, Vintage, 1969, Volume 2, pp. 205, 213–214.
43 Cited in Parkinson, Roger, *The Origins of World War II*, Wayland, 1970, p. 17.
44 Cited *inter alia* by Lowe, N., *Mastering Modern World History*, Macmillan, 1982, p. 8.

Index

Figures in **bold** refer to illustrations

Aehrenthal 19, 57
Africa **14**,
    scramble for 14
Agadir **30**
Albania 34, 37
Algeciras Conference 19, 23, 25, 56
Alliance of the Three Emperors 6, **50**, 56
Austria–Hungary 15, 16, 29, 30, 34, 35, 37, 39
    agreement with Russia 26, 56
    Alliance of the Three Emperors 6, 56
    Bosnia and Herzegovina 4, 19, 26, 28, 30, 41,
        51, 53, 57
    Mediterranean Agreement 7, 56
    Triple Alliance 6-7, 18, 56
    war with Serbia 5, 27, 38, 40, 43, 57
Asquith, H. H. 33, **53**, 54

Balkan League 26-7, 57
    see also Greece; Serbia; Montenegro; Bulgaria
Balkan Wars 26-7, 32-5, **34**, 50, 57
Balkans 9, 15, 26-37, **28, 33**
Belgium 39, 44, **45**
Berchtold, Count Leopold 40, 54
Bismarck, Otto von 6-7, **7**, 8, **22**, 25, 42, **50**, 56
Black Hand gang 4
Boer War 10, 18, 20, 56
Bosnia 4, 19, 26, 28, 30, 41, 51, 53, 57
Britain 10-11, 29, 35, 39, 44, 48, 51
    alliance with Japan 18, 21, 36, 56
    Boer War 10, 18, 20, 56
    declares war on Germany 39
    economy 10, 12-13
    Entente Cordiale 18, 22-3, 25, 32, 36, 56
    Fashoda crisis 10, 15, **15**, 56
    free trade 12-13
    isolation 11, 18, 21
    Mediterranean Agreement 7, 56
    naval agreement with France 36, 57
    navy 17, 19, 26, 30, 52
    relations with Russia 11, 19, **20**, 24, **24**, 35, 36,
        57
Buchlau agreement 57
Bulgaria 26, 27, 28, 34-5, 39, 57

Chamberlain, Joseph 12, **15**, 21
China 15
    Manchuria occupied by Russia 18, 20, 56
Churchill, Winston 17
Congress of Berlin 56
Congress of Vienna 56
Crimean War 10, **10**, 22, 56

Dreadnought, HMS 17, **17**, 56
Dual Alliance 8-9, 16, 20
    see also France; Russia

Edward VII 18, **18**, 21, 23
Egypt 10, 15, 22, 23
Entente Cordiale 18, 22-3, 25, 32, 56

Fashoda crisis 10, 15, **15**, 22, 56
Fisher, Sir John 19, 54
France 8, 16, 22-3, 29, 36-7, 41, 48, 52-3
    alliance with Russia 7, 8-9, 36, 56
    Germany declares war 38
    defeated by Prussia 6-7, **6**, 22, 51, 56
    Entente Cordiale 18, 22-3, 25, 32, 36, 56
    Fashoda crisis 10, 15, **15**, 56
    naval agreement with Britain 36, 57
    treaty with Italy 18, 56
Franz Josef, Emperor **40**, 54
Fanz Ferdinand, Archduke 4, **4**, 27, 38, **49, 51**,
    57
Free trade 12-13

Germany 6-7, 20, 25, 35, 43, 48-9, 51, 52-3
    Alliance of the Three Emperors 6, 56
    army 16-17, 23
    declares war on France 38, 57
    declares war on Russia 38, 39, 57
    economy 9, 10, 13
    German Empire proclaimed 8, **8**, 56
    Triple Alliance 6-7, 18, 56
    Navy Laws 11, 17, 18, 19, 32, 56, 57
    preparation for war **33**, 37, 42
Greece 26, 27, 28, 34, 39, 47, 56, 57
Grey, Sir Edward 16, 17, 23, 24, **25**, 33, 34, 35,
    44, 54

Haldane, Lord 26, 33, 57
Herzegovina 19, 26, 28, 30, 41, 51, 53, 57

Italy 7, 15, 29, 37, 39, 46-7
    Mediterranean Agreement 7, 56
    treaty with France 18, 56
    Triple Alliance 7, 16, 18, 56
    war with Turkey 26, **27**, 57
Izvolsky, Alexander 19, 55, 57

Japan 39, 57
    treaty with Britain 18, 21, 36, 56
    war with Russia 18, **19**, 56

Libya 26

Lloyd George, David 26, 31, 57
London Conference of Ambassadors 34, 35

Mediterranean Agreement 7, 56
Moltke, General Helmuth von 37, **37**, 42-3, 55
Montenegro 26, 28, 34, 35, 38, 57
Morocco 19, 21, **21**, 23, 25, 26, 30, 31, **35**, 36-7, **48**, 52-3

Napoleon I 8, **51**, 56
Napoleon III 8, 56
Nicholas II, Czar **9**, 18, 24, **25**, 56

Portugal 39
Princip, Gavrilo 4, **4**, 52
Prussia 6, 56

Romania 27, 28, 34, 39, 56, 57
Russia 9, 15, 16, 29, 30, 35, 38, 43, 47, 50, 53
    agreement with Austria 26, 56
    Alliance of the Three Emperors 6, 56
    alliance with France 7, 8-9, 36, 41, 56
    Germany declares war 38
    occupation of Manchuria 18, 20, 56
    relations with Britain 11, 19, **20, 21**, 24, 35, 36, 56, 57
    war with Japan 18, **19**, 56
    1905 Revolution 18, 56

Salisbury, Lord 20

Sarajevo 4, 57
Sazonov, Sergei 25, 31, 37
Schlieffen, Alfred von 19, 42
Schlieffen Plan 42-3, **43**, 52, 56
Scutari 34
Serbia 4, **5**, 28, **29**, 34-5, 40, 47, 50, 53
    Balkan League 26, 57
    Balkan Wars **26**, 27, 57
    war with Austria 5, 27, 38, 40, 57
Suez Canal 11, **32**

Tirpitz, Admiral von **17**, 18, 55
Treaty of London 27, 39, 44, 56, 57
Treaty of Versailles 48
Triple Alliance 6-7, 16, 18, 25, 57
    see also Germany; Austria; Italy
Triple Entente 37, 57
Turkey 27, 28-9, 34-5, 39, 56, 57

U-Boats **27, 53**
United States 20, **38, 47**, 48
    declares war on Germany 39, 47, 57

Victor Emmanuel III **7**
Victoria, Queen 10, **11**

William II, Kaiser 7, 18, 21, **22**, 23, **23**, 30, **30**, 40, 43, **46**, 55, 56
Wilson, President Woodrow 47